COME BACK SAM, ALL IS FORGIVEN

# COME BACK SAM, ALL IS FORGIVEN

Goff Mason-Apps

The Book Guild Ltd.
Sussex, England

This book is sold subject to the condition that it shall not, by way of trade or otherwise, be lent, re-sold, hired out, photocopied or held in any retrieval system or otherwise circulated without the publisher's prior consent in any form of binding or cover other than that in which this is published and without a similar condition including this condition being imposed on the subsequent purchaser.

The Book Guild Ltd.
25 High Street,
Lewes, Sussex

First published 1997
© Goff Mason-Apps, 1997

Set in Times

Typesetting by Raven Typesetters, Chester

Printed in Great Britain by
Antony Rowe Ltd. Chippenham, Wiltshire.

A catalogue record for this book is
available from the British Library

ISBN 1 85776 150 2

*A Yorkshire Terrier's Lament* – on being told to be quiet and stop annoying the neighbours

With apologies to W. H. Davies

What is this life if (for a lark)
We have no time to stand and bark?

No time to stand in morning sun,
And make the children scream and run;

To chase them till they turn around –
Then hastily retrace our ground;

To bark at girl and bark at boy –
To bark for unrestricted joy;

To bark at road and bark at wall –
(To bark, at times, at nowt\* at all!)

To stand by gate and *bark* and *bark* –
To mark our ground and make our mark.

What is this life if (just for a lark)
We have no time to stand – and bark?

\*(I am, after all, a Yorkshire terrier)

Previously published in *The Dalesman*, March 1992

# INTRODUCTION

Although during our first acquaintance with Sam – at a remote kennels where my mother and I had gone to look at a potential birthday present for her – we had become aware of warning signs, we decided to override them. After all, he *was* a Yorkshire terrier and as such fulfilled the main part of her long held desire. Also in his favour was his scruffy, friendly appeal. Perhaps the greatest point though, and the reason we were there, was the fact that the price advertised in the local newspaper was sufficiently less than that generally demanded for Yorkshire terrier puppies as to make the difference between affordability and not. There, however, lay the key to the problem.

Sam, though still a puppy, was ten months old. Whatever had happened in those ten months seemed to have left an indelible mark on him, leaving him a mass of neuroses, of varying complexity. He also failed to conform to our expectation in regard to size – seeming relatively large and boisterous by comparison with our image of dainty 'prettiness'. He was not a 'Toy', on which our image was based, but a 'Standard'. Dainty and pretty were the last words that came to mind at the time! The fact that later on we wouldn't have considered changing him – certainly not for one of those effeminate-seeming creatures – didn't affect our response then. He was not what we expected.

Perhaps it's as well that we didn't appreciate just what we were letting ourselves in for when we fell then for his apparent open innocence – the same innocence that seems to shine through in later photographs. If we had, we would probably have rejected him and never have known what we had missed. Without Sam, our lives would have been immeasurably impoverished. His very perversity and 'naughtiness' made him what he was: in the very least, a distraction and respite from the worries of everyday life. I have only recently begun fully to take in his most important contribution – the difference he must have made to my mother's life, particularly in her later years. Generally an unhappy time for her, without Sam, this unhappiness would perhaps have been unendurable. Right at the end, lying as usual on her bed, he resisted with snarling fury the efforts of the ambulancemen to take her away. It was only her calming words that enabled the operation to be carried out.

Although at best, people tended to tolerate him and, more usually, to be more aware of his faults than anything else, he did have his fans. Amongst these were the taxi-drivers who occasionally conveyed him to the local boarding-kennels when I had to go away, with whom he enjoyed a positively angelic reputation. Again, the young man whose family later took Sam in on these occasions reported with some disgust how friends when calling tended to push past *him* to greet and fuss over Sam. His sister, also, on returning from work, made straight for Sam to put him on his lead and take him out. At the end of one visit, she had asked: 'He will be coming for Christmas again, won't he?' I should think though that Sam's greatest fans ought to have been the bluebottles to whom he took on the self-appointed role of protector from my furious assaults with rolled-up newspaper.

What I feel must be conceded is that, when all is added

up, he gave more to us than we to him. While expecting instant forgiveness for even the most outrageous of his acts, he also bestowed it without hesitation. Though it had taken an off-hand remark by a friend of my mother to call to my attention the importance Sam was assuming in my life, well before the end it became obvious – to a degree that was borne out by my reaction to his death. So much so, that, as the front door closed a couple of days later behind an ex-colleague who had been comforting me, I suddenly felt so aware of my bereavement that I found myself crying out: 'Don't leave me, Sam! Don't leave me! I can't live without you!' with such pent-up emotion that I thought that the departing friend must hear me. Still now, I am haunted intermittently by the image of his little face peering expectantly through the glass panel in the front door on his being brought back from someone else's care.

Come back, Sam! All is forgiven!

I suppose you could say that, as I inherited Sam from my mother, it therefore served me right. After all, I *had* bought him – for her birthday, a few years before she died. She had always wanted a Yorkshire terrier, she had said. Mind you, what she had really wanted was a young puppy but what few were available at that time were priced beyond my means. We ended up going to see a dog of ten months advertised by a remote kennels – not cheap but just about affordable. We were both thinking in terms of a 'toy', or very small, dainty-looking, animal. What appeared, though undoubtedly a Yorkshire terrier and small by normal standards, didn't by any means conform with this image. My impression was of a great, scruffy thing, which on release tore around the kennels' front lawn, leapt a couple of times over a centrally placed statuette, and relieved himself rather ostentatiously. 'See how house-trained he is!' cried the proprietress. 'He's been holding that till now!'

Regarding him with some misgiving as he stood before us, we were influenced in his favour by a) his apparent open, eager friendliness; and b) the fact that the kennels weren't prepared to compromise over the price of their small puppies. However, even before we decided, there had been warning signs: the statement that he mustn't go where there were young children; and, seemingly unconnected, his age. It appeared obvious later that, not only was there a connection, but that it was his age at purchase that was the crucial factor affecting Sam's psychology.

We soon found that, not only did Sam hate being picked up, but he also hated having anyone bend over him – in each case responding with snarling and snapping. Taking this together with the evident tenderness of his ribs and the proviso stated above about young children, we came to suspect that in those first ten months he had been roughly handled by a young family member who, in trying to pick him up, had hurt him and been bitten. I think it most likely that Sam was then pretty severely beaten. Certainly, he still tends to get very nervous and upset when he hears young voices outside and even more when children come into the house.

The more we got to know about him, the more we began to feel that the kennels weren't being entirely honest with us – there was something to hide. We were told that the reason for the previous owners' decision to get rid of him was that they were selling up and going to America, which seemed reasonable on the surface. However, the fact that in his vaccination card the name 'Toby' had been overwritten to change it to 'Toy' (which he wasn't anyway, being the larger 'Standard') appeared suspicious to say the least. We vaguely considered following this up by attempting to get in touch with the woman in Farnham whose name appeared as owner on the card, but never did.

Gradually, the extent of his neuroses began to be borne in upon us; as for instance his hatred of whistling and of motor-horns, both of which sent him in to paroxysms of wild barking. He hated too, both scissors and sprays – the mere sight of either in one's hand again provoking snarling and snapping, followed by his rushing to hide behind the sofa or in my mother's bedroom. Even his spotting something that his suspicious mind could interpret as one or the other produced the same reaction. This made any attempt at grooming him or keeping him clear of fleas almost impossible to achieve. Hairdriers seemed to cause him most distress – both the noise and the feel of the wind, I suppose – so any drying after a bath had to be done by hand. Although the reaction to whistling and motor-horns has gradually been reduced with time, any hope that this was a manifestation of a general mellowing have in the main been dashed as more inhibitions have been revealed and his behaviour has steadily become more bizarre.

Sam soon made it clear that he considered that anything that upset him or caused him any hurt was done deliberately – by the human being who happened to be nearest to him at the time! Thus, not only did he not restrict himself to squealing when trodden on – attacking the leg of the offender instead – but, on being roused from slumber by the ringing of the telephone (another hated noise), launched himself with much sound and fury at the ankles of the person he considered responsible – the poor unfortunate who tried to cross the room to answer it.

His semi-permanent state of inner-tension seemed to me to be highlighted by his behaviour outside when passing water. Except on those occasions when he had been deprived of the opportunity of relief for some time – as on our first encounter with him – Sam tended to cock his leg, give a little dribble, walk a short distance, cock his leg, give another dribble, walk a little further, and so on. One got the impression at the end of this performance that he still had not emptied his bladder fully. He appeared unable to relax sufficiently.

Actually, he seemed to settle in to his new home quite naturally, though he showed his objection to being shut in the kitchen at night, scratching the door and barking, causing me to have to go down to him. I felt it important, however, that we should try to get him used to it. After all, having been previously in the company of other dogs, it was inevitable that he would initially feel unhappy at being suddenly shut in alone. Although I tried to convince my mother to leave him – he would soon come to accept it – she decided on only the second or third night to take him upstairs with her; '...just until he settles down!'

In fact, of course, once he had been allowed upstairs that was it. From then on, Sam always made sure he was up there first; the moment the living-room door was opened in late evening he would be through it, racing up the stairs. If the door to my mother's bedroom was open, he would be inside, either on the bed or hiding under it. If it was closed, he would be waiting outside. She soon had to accept that trying to force him down again just wasn't on. Sam ended up in the bedroom, either on the bed or, sometimes, *in* it.

Before long we were to realise that we had inherited another problem relating to those ten months before we had him, as it became evident that, not only had Sam been trained not to do anything in the house but also, that even the garden was off-limits for a 'job'. My mother had assumed that on those days when she was unable to take him out she could just let him into the back garden to carry out his normal bodily functions. But no; the brainwashing had obviously been very successful. Whilst in extremes he was prepared to 'cock his leg', it was thus far and no further. When we moved to a larger house with a rather larger rear garden where my mother hoped he would be prepared to do everything, he still staunchly resisted the temptation.

After my mother died, a colleague with a very big semi-wild country garden in which she kept chickens, geese, and other livestock, kindly took Sam over while I was in hospital. As these animals mostly seemed to roam fairly freely, 'doing what comes naturally', I more or less took it for granted, as did, apparently my friend, that here at least Sam would have no inhibitions and would do the same. It wasn't until much later that his host revealed in passing that to her surprise, '... he insisted on being taken out before he would do anything!'

Unfortunately, this ingrained characteristic meant that on those days when my mother was unable to take Sam out, and this tended to happen more and more frequently as she became increasingly frail with age, she felt forced just to let him out the front. As Sam's hang-ups were revealed as being restricted to the property in which he was presently living, he, and my mother, became somewhat unpopular with the neighbours. One fellow protested that the moment Sam was let out he went straight across the road and did a job in the middle of his driveway!

When Sam suddenly became *my* responsibility, it was obvious that I had to find someone to take him for walks. I myself was ruled out because not only was I teaching during the day, but, as one result of childhood polio, was small, light and becoming increasingly uncertain on my feet. Though a small dog, Sam's sudden jerks on the lead were sufficient to cause me to lose my balance.

Two teenaged girls were engaged to take him to a local green and told to take him off the lead there and let him run around, as my mother used to on the occasions that she took him out. Sam soon demonstrated his perversity. Apparently, the moment he was released he turned tail and made off home. It became difficult after the first two occasions to get him to go at all. They started off having to drag him. Soon, he began to hide the moment he heard them at the door and any attempt to retrieve him was met with his usual snarling and snapping. It was eventually abandoned as an obvious lost cause.

Some years later a newly acquired friend, also a retired teacher who had taken up writing, offered to walk him.

Very much affected by the recent loss of his wife, he seemed to take to Sam and Sam to him. To what extent this was influenced, in Sam's case, by the fact that on each visit a chocolate biscuit tended to be produced from this stranger's pocket, I don't know, but it seemed almost ideal. Besides solving the problem that was beginning to appear insoluble in regard to Sam's exercise and getting rid of body waste, it also appeared useful for George, as although his motivation was almost certainly principally kindness, I felt that he was genuinely looking forward to the idea of these excursions as a pleasant additional way of taking his mind off things. It seemed to me accordingly that he was quite deeply hurt when Sam, after initially trotting off happily with him, then reverted to his previous behaviour, hiding and snarling at any attempt to put him on his lead.

From this time it was almost impossible to get him to accept the lead, unless he thought he was going out in the car, which he loved. This led to a not-to-be-forgotten incident when Sam was due to be collected for a much-needed trim. Because on the previous occasion he had gone through his usual routine of hiding, causing the woman to have to come back again later (with resulting extra charge), I decided, by means of much subterfuge, to have him ready on his lead overnight.

The moment I opened my bedroom door in the morning I was hit by the smell! Exactly what had set it all off I don't know – perhaps he was worried and/or excited at finding himself on the lead? However, at some stage in the night he had got himself trapped in what had been my mother's downstairs bedroom and had done a job. A large part of this had got stuck in the over-long fur around his rear end and had then been smeared around the walls. To add to the mayhem, in his panic he had knocked over and broken a leg off a bedside table. When I arrived he was still trying to extricate himself.

Now, the trouble was that there was little time before he was due to be collected. I knew there was no way that I could get him cleaned up in time and frankly wouldn't even have liked to attempt it, but I thought it even more imperative now that he should be trimmed. I couldn't bear the idea of putting it off for another time and having to go through it all again. I took my courage in my hands and rang the groomer, telling her honestly what a state Sam was in and hoping she would still accept the challenge. With some reluctance, she did – after I promised to wrap him in a towel. Even then, when she saw and smelt him, she involuntarily stepped back a couple of paces! His trim turned out to be not far short of a crew cut, but in the circumstances, I didn't feel I could complain. She said she had to ask for an extra £5 but I had already decided it would have to be an extra £10. The important thing as far as I was concerned was to try to ensure that she would be prepared to take him again!

He constituted a considerable problem when I had to go away. The first time I was admitted to Brompton Hospital in London, an elderly friend of my mother, who had already been very kind to Sam and me, volunteered to have him till I returned. Having previously taken the precaution of telling her to send him by taxi to a nearby kennels if anything went wrong, I suppose I shouldn't have been surprised when I received a letter after less than a week apologising for the fact that, both the friend and *her* friend having been bitten within the space of 24 hours she had felt constrained to do just that. Ah well!

In anticipation of future needs, and bearing in mind the cost of kennels, I decided to place an advertisement in the window of a local newsagent. The thinking behind the careful wording was a) if anything happened, they couldn't say they hadn't been warned! and b) in a kind of reverse psychology, I felt the catalogue of his faults might sufficiently amuse and intrigue people as to draw them to him and cause them to decide to take him on – if only to see if he could possibly be that bad!

It ran thus:

> Kind home, without young children, sought for scruffy, smelly, disobedient, bad tempered, Yorkshire terrier, while disabled owner is on holiday.
> Telephone: ------

I felt compelled though to add: (He's quite lovable, really!)

After some days, having had no response, I rang the newsagent to ask if there had been any reaction. He said it had been a source of great amusement. People had been gathering around the shop window, pointing it out to each other, then coming inside and laughing and joking about it. Did anyone offer to take him on? Well, no – but they thought it a great joke!

It was shortly after this that the colleague with the large garden and the animals volunteered to have him when necessary. When I enquired anxiously on his return if he had been any trouble, I was assured he'd been none at all – most of the time they'd hardly known he'd been there! It wasn't until some time later that I discovered that apart from the minor misdemeanour of rejecting his own food in favour of that put out for their cat, he'd caused them to spend the early part of many nights having to use a broomhandle to get him out from under their bed! When you add to this the disclosure by the same informant that Sam's hostess didn't like dogs anyway, it really does seem to be a case of devotion over and above the call of duty! Certainly, it's a kindness for which I shall feel eternally grateful. No one else at that time would even consider offering to take him.

One of Sam's most extraordinary quirks of behaviour didn't appear until after our move to this present house and seems to relate to the disposition of our large three-piece suite! The sofa on which he tended to spend a lot of his time dozing is placed against the wall to the right of my armchair. One evening, seemingly waking with a start, he leapt up, bounded across the room, and grabbed my left foot – snarling and shaking it as if it were a rat. When I tried to dislodge him by lifting that leg he hung on the tighter, still snarling and shaking, as he was suspended from my foot. After a while, apparently feeling rather silly, he slowly let go and ambled shamefacedly back to the sofa.

What the meaning of this was, I don't know – perhaps it was as we thought at the time, that he'd woken suddenly from a dream in which some small animal posed a threat and this had then been identified in his mind with my foot. However, the more often this performance is repeated – and it is, periodically, the less likely this seems. The fact that it is always my left foot – on the opposite side from where he is lying – is an added peculiarity. While these constant attacks were bad enough – resulting in a hole appearing in the toe of the left foot of my favourite pair of slippers – the real crunch came on the couple of times when the sudden arrival of Sam's teeth coincided with my slipper-less feet being protected only by thin socks!

His behaviour in the first few years we had him was very much that of a very small child – wherever he was, he wanted to be somewhere else! If he was up he wanted to be down. If he was in one chair he would suddenly decide he wanted to be in another. If he was inside he wanted to be out. This again seemed to become most evident after our move and was, I feel, encouraged by my mother's desire to keep him happy. It got to a stage where she would be constantly jumping up and down to let him into the kitchen or out the front in response to his least indication of need – real or apparent. It did *my* nerves very little good, whatever it did for Sam.

As being bathed is universally resisted by dogs, it can be imagined that Sam was no exception. However, once he had been persuaded to accept being put on his lead (not, with Sam, the easiest thing!) the problem was much reduced. Though, inevitably, he tended to hold back when he realised what was going on, he allowed himself to be led in to the bathroom and put in a rectangular plastic bowl intended originally for washing-up, but just the right size for him.

It is typical of his contradictory nature that after a half-hearted attempt to get out he seemed to accept his fate, standing there shivering and looking miserable as water was poured over him and dog-shampoo rubbed in. This was a new Sam in other ways too – soaked with water and with his skin clinging tightly to him he looked so small and thin and vulnerable; more like a chihuahua than a Yorkshire terrier. Of course though, in getting out he managed to get his own back – soaking everyone in the vicinity. Even wearing a thick plastic apron hardly saved me. The one thing he did seem to enjoy was being towelled dry afterwards, liking to jump on what was my mother's bed for it to be done there. While this obviously was not ideal, it made it much easier for the person doing the drying. The difficulty was in getting him to stand still long enough to do it properly.

One positive factor against all the negative ones that impressed itself upon me in those early days was his tendency to rush up to the door barking when he heard anything there. Both the postman and the newsboy got an instant angry reception. When you added to this his furious protest at the sight of anyone daring to walk past on the pavement in front of the house – invading *his* territory

— one hoped the word would get around the neighbourhood that the house held a very noisy dog; thus deterring any potential burglar.

This comfortable, and comfort*ing*, image lasted until one morning I suddenly realised the post had come without any reaction from Sam, who was curled up on the sofa oblivious. It soon became obvious he barked now only when *he* felt like it! This became more and more infrequent as time went by, only the sound of the evening paper dropping through the letter-box continuing to provoke any kind of a consistent response. Even this, I suspect, was more to do with its association in his mind with a young newsboy than anything else. Gradually, his tendency still to rush to the door on hearing anyone there became based solely on his own curiosity to discover who it was. On most occasions visitors are made to feel welcome! The strange thing — though perhaps again typical of his contradictions — is the fact that even in later years when his sight was failing he continued his angry protest at seeing people passing in front of the house.

It was entirely consistent with everything else about him that he had soon shown himself to be a problem in regard to feeding. We tried as far as possible to get him fresh meat from the butcher but it was difficult to find suitable meat that was also reasonably priced. He rejected 'pet-mince' out of hand. Tinned dog-food he seemed also to feel unacceptable, except in extreme circumstances. While he did deign sometimes to eat a little from a freshly opened can, that was it; he wasn't prepared to consider anything more from the same tin. No matter how often it was brought out and put before him, he tended just to give it a quick glance, sometimes a sniff, then turn away. My mother decided that a canned food supposedly formulated especially for small dogs might be the answer. Unfortunately, his response to this was just the same;

although it was a small can, he ate less than half and refused later to look at the rest. As this can turned out to be as expensive as one twice the size, this experiment was abandoned.

He also rejected dog-biscuits, whether given separately or mixed with his other food. Because we felt they were an important part of a dog's normal diet we tried breaking them up, thinking they were perhaps too large to be handled easily by his small mouth. It made little or no difference — still they were left on his plate. We then tried softening them with water or gravy (though this seemed to defeat at least part of the object — that of giving exercise to his teeth and jaw) but again, to no avail. He showed no interest in bones even when they had a little meat left on them, so that alternative means of keeping his teeth healthy was also out. However, as the local PDSA vet had strongly advised against dogs being given *any kind* of bones, as he claimed he had to deal with more cases of stomachs being pierced by bone fragments than almost anything else, perhaps that was not a bad thing.

For a while, it seemed that these problems had gone some way towards being solved. A type of biscuit I discovered — allegedly containing marrowbone — he appeared to quite take to, crunching it with what seemed enjoyment. This didn't last though. Soon he generally ignored them; only rarely, by standing with his nose pressed against the cupboard where they were kept, did he indicate any interest. Even then, as often as not, when he was given one he would just abandon it on the kitchen floor!

Again, a kind of 'dog-sausage' which I was recommended but of which I had little hope he greeted initially with surprising enthusiasm, wolfing down the tentative first offering then turning round looking for more. This enthusiasm, however, — inevitably with Sam — wore off and it became a case of trying to get by, alternating the sausage with the canned meat. A lot, though, tended to get wasted. My own view was that he would eat it if he was hungry and I had little patience in those early years when my mother started opening a can of corned-beef for him, feeling sure he would almost certainly waste most of that. Unfortunately, when put to the test of hunger Sam showed himself to be quite prepared to go for 48 hours or more without touching the food put down for him! It got a little worrying, particularly to my mother. The trouble was that it was a no-win situation in that generally there was nothing to replace it with.

He had it in common with other dogs though, that he usually enjoyed any scraps from our table, following out expectantly as the plates were taken through to the kitchen after a meal. If he had his own food still left on his dish, I began to try to make it clear to him that he wouldn't get anything until he had eaten that. Often I would then more or less forget it, getting on with other things in the kitchen and would suddenly become aware of Sam darting back and forth between me and his dish. Sometimes he actually nudged my leg with his nose to draw my attention. As often as not he would then stand with his back to me in front of his dish, looking over his shoulder, as if to ask, 'Is that good enough?' Once or twice he had actually cleared everything, more often he had just eaten a little – sometimes he would take a quick gulp while I watched, then turn around to see my reaction.

Obviously, if he had eaten it all I would give him everything there was, going out of my way to pat and praise him. If only part, I tried to persevere to get him to finish it, though as often as not he would get it eventually. Unfortunately, on many occasions I found afterwards that he had dumped a large part of the food I thought he had cleared, on to the kitchen floor – I often discovered it by treading on it!

When being 'encouraged' to eat something he didn't approve of he made a great play of this dislike, taking a quick mouthful, and, with much shaking of the head, dumping it on the floor. He would then pick it up again, shake his head again, and repeat. Watching him, one would get the impression that he was being asked to eat something absolutely disgusting! Sometimes, so convincing was he, that I picked up his dish to check by smell if it had gone off. I must admit that on one or two rare occasions it had (as a result of his pig-headedly refusing to touch it) but generally it was fine. Sam was nothing if not a fine actor.

Of course, there *were* things besides the remains of our own meals that he enjoyed but most of them had been introduced to him via our plates; for instance, bacon – which he worshipped. He also liked cooked tomatoes, though my mother tended to worry that the skins might not be good for him. I would say though that bacon's only serious competitors in the Sam popularity stakes were sausages. Whenever they were being cooked he would be hovering around as close to one's feet as he dared. Usually, I would try to cook at least one extra for him, which I would cut up and add to anything I had not eaten. I must admit I often then put it all on top of any food he had left on his dish in the hope that he would then eat it all. Sometimes it worked – more usually it didn't. When he turned away, having carefully sorted out the pieces of sausage, the previously rejected food was still there.

He sometimes enjoyed cheese, though this was only revealed when bits of grated cheese were dropped on the kitchen floor when preparing Welsh rarebit. His liking for apple peel was discovered in the same way, as was his, perhaps more surprising, enjoyment of the cores! When he first grabbed one as it fell at my feet, I tried to snatch it back, thinking it couldn't be good for his stomach.

However, having almost lost my hand in the process, I let him keep it. Noting the great relish with which he set about it, I decided to continue offering them to him, reminding myself that this was, in the least, exercise for his teeth and jaw. The doubt I felt about the possible effect on his stomach I pushed to the back of my mind.

If his liking for apple peel and cores was a little unusual, it was not, I think, worthy of the surprise with which I received the next revelation. Standing at the kitchen sink one evening peeling the potatoes, with Sam, his usual inquisitive self, standing behind me, I was suddenly aware of a crunching noise. Turning, I saw Sam chomping on a piece of peel that had evidently fallen. The fact that he was doing it with such relish encouraged me to drop him a couple more pieces – more than half-expecting him to reject them, now they were actually being *offered* to him. He attacked them with as much enthusiasm as the first. Needing no further encouragement, I grabbed a handful, rinsed them this time under the tap, and put them on his dish.

For the next few minutes I stood at the sink watching and listening to him as he crunched away, alternately burying his head in the dish and looking round at me. His enjoyment was so obvious it conveyed itself to *me*. I found it very pleasing that I had found, if only by accident, an addition to his diet that seemed to so please him. My feeling too was that, as with, apparently, a dog's tendency at times to eat grass, this perhaps revealed some dietary need being filled. On that first occasion, I think I added at least two more handfuls to his dish.

From that time this became a regular performance. Whenever I was peeling potatoes, or Sam thought I was, he would be behind me waiting his share. While at times, perhaps inevitably, some would end up abandoned on the kitchen floor, in the main he continued to eat and enjoy them, crunching away happily as before. The advent of the new-potato season obviously confused him, as he saw me at the sink with potatoes but then nothing emerged for him. Belatedly, it did occur to me to cut a few slivers off the scraped flesh for him, but I must admit that on most occasions I forgot.

Whilst I had come to accept his getting on the furniture, allowing it to continue after the death of my mother – against my better judgement – I tried to restrict it to the sofa as much as possible. I particularly tried to keep him off the other armchair, whose loose cover remained virtually unsullied. There were times too – particularly at night – when I wanted to keep him off my chair. However, he proved almost impossible to deter, seeming to have an in-built tendency, and desire, to get where he wasn't wanted.

The other armchair ought not to have been especially inviting to him, piled high as it generally tends to be with papers, magazines, letters and various other things dumped there to be out of the way, with the vague idea of their being dealt with later. (Perhaps I should be honest and admit that the same applies to a large part of the sofa – and various other pieces of furniture, my not being the tidiest, most organised person in the world.) However, time without number I would suddenly become aware of Sam standing tensed in front of that chair, nose pointing up and bottom wiggling as he prepared to launch himself. Sometimes I managed to divert him by shouting, though this was usually only a temporary respite before he had another go. Often, my first awareness would be the sound of crushing newspaper as he actually landed. I then, besides clearing him off again, had to try to ascertain what, if any, damage he had done. Always, amongst the apparently abandoned mess were items – manuscripts, letters – I needed to protect.

At times, especially when he has been ill and I have had

to put paper down in the hall in case he felt forced to do a job in the night, keeping him down from the armchairs became particularly important as, on returning from such a trip, he tended to soil them. However, although I went so far as to put a rectangularly shaped plywood board and two crossed walking-sticks across my chair before I went to bed, as often as not I went into the living-room the next morning to find Sam perched precariously on top.

Now, this board had been finely sanded and polished to facilitate its use in one of my leg exercises. Sometimes I heard a thump in the night which, on discovering the board now leaning off the front of the chair-cushion like a ski-ramp and Sam now elsewhere, I concluded was the sound of him being projected off. As often as not, though, I found in the morning that, having initially clambered aboard, he had then managed to pull my large cushion down from the back of the chair and was now nestling high and mighty on top of that – in turn, on top of the plywood and the sticks! Sam was determined not to be thwarted!

As in so many things, in his choice of resting-place he presented something of a paradox; while generally he would seek the most obviously comfortable spot – when in either chair eventually pulling down the cushion and clambering on it – often he would seem to go to the other extreme. An example of this occurred when, after putting some boxes in the space between the sofa and the other armchair, I was suddenly aware that Sam was nowhere to be seen. Eventually, he was discovered fast asleep, having somehow clambered on to them. The fact that they were of an awkward size (the upper surface of the one he was resting on being smaller than he was) and of very stiff cardboard, seemed to offer no deterrence.

Not only had he got used to sitting in the armchairs but also to deciding exactly *where* in the chair, expecting any human occupant to move out of the way as he burrowed into his chosen spot. My mother, under mild protest, invariably did so as Sam, by wriggling and pushing, gradually increased *his* space and reduced my mother's. On the rare occasions while she was still alive that he decided he wanted to sit with me, he found me less compliant – largely because he always opted for the left-hand side of the seat, which was the most comfortable side for me. If he was allowed to stay, it was on the right-hand side, where he made it obvious he wasn't happy!

Perhaps not surprisingly, he had become more and more my mother's dog – not just literally now but also psychologically. When there was any verbal dispute he began to stand between us, confronting me, snarling and barking. Even now, years after her death, if I suddenly exclaim 'Oh my God!' Sam will be on his feet in front of me in an instant, barking wildly. This expression had often been the precursor of an argument involving Sam and my mother on one side and me on the other.

This situation, by which I seemed to have become established in Sam's mind almost as 'the enemy', perhaps goes some way towards explaining another recently revealed aspect of his behaviour – his apparent self-appointed role of defender of flies. On taking up a rolled-up newspaper to attempt to bring to book a particularly worrisome bluebottle, I found Sam leaping and snapping as he tried to thwart me. Soon, I was left with just a shredded stump as his newly acquired six-legged friend made good his escape to the far corner of the room. The fact that on the occasions when this occurs I usually discover too late that the paper involved was either one I hadn't read or had wanted for some reason to keep, tends not to improve my temper.

(Of course, my occasional use of a rolled-up newspaper to clout Sam himself may also have played some part in his feeling of empathy towards what he probably regards as fellow creatures under attack by the common enemy.)

He has a tendency not to accept physical punishment lightly but to fight back, snarling and biting, when, for instance, hit with the lead. Although I am sure this is something which dog experts, and others, will say shouldn't be allowed, *saying* that is very easy. Stopping it, with Sam, is something else. At least though, rationalising, it could be said he is not cowed! He has, I suppose, done what we are told dogs should never be able to do – that is, decide that he is the equal of human beings. Or is it just me and my mother before me?

Now, following an incident in which he was being held by the collar and struck with the lead for making a pool on the hall carpet straight after being let in from an outing intended for him to relieve himself, he very seldom *is* physically punished. On that occasion, I suddenly became aware that he was crouching down on his haunches. Before I could react he had done a job – this time, on the living-room carpet! My first response had been of increased anger but this was quickly replaced by compassion, as I realised the implication – he was obviously terrified. In fact, when I got back from taking him outside again, I discovered that, in the time taken to move him he had done two more jobs! Nowadays, I tend to limit myself to verbal chastisement.

Perhaps surprisingly, considering his general apparent lack of concern, Sam has, by his response on two occasions, shown himself to hate being made to feel unpopular. Shortly before she died, my mother had told me how the previous night Sam had really frightened her. I can't recall exactly what she said had happened but Sam, on her bed as usual, had done something to which she objected and she had shouted at him, told him he was a bad dog, and, she said, obviously still shaken, 'I really thought he was going to attack me!'

This was brought back to me some months later. Again, I can't quite remember exactly what Sam had done, but I had found it necessary to tell him off severely, probably shouting at him. Sam was on the floor by my chair. Suddenly he leapt onto my lap, thrusting his head in to my face and snarling. Apprehensive, with thoughts of what my mother had told me forced into my mind, I was concerned not to do anything that might precipitate the attack. Then, something about his behaviour – the *kind* of noise he was making – made me realise that this wasn't a threatened attack, but a demand for forgiveness! I wondered afterwards if this was the explanation behind the incident with my mother. Certainly, when I stroked Sam and comforted him, he settled down quietly on my lap.

A particularly strange and worrying aspect of his behaviour that appeared a few years ago involved such things as sudden flinching, as if fearing a blow, shivering – again, as if frightened – and hiding. He would, in the latter case disappear behind the sofa, occasionally putting just his head out to peer, seemingly apprehensive, around. No amount of coaxing would persuade him out. He remained there until he himself decided he was ready – the coast being clear; the danger gone? In none of these cases was there any obvious cause. Although the flinching and shivering first appeared immediately following a period when he was being looked after by someone else, I cannot believe that it was anything they did that could have brought about this reaction. Perhaps the only possibility is that something was done by another person when he was out of their sight. It could of course be just another manifestation of his general neurotic state. I worried though that other people, witnessing this behaviour, might tend to assume that it was due to ill-treatment, by me.

It is another characteristic of his that, whatever he has done; however strongly it has been made clear to him that he has done wrong, he expects to be forgiven immediately. Whether it is that his memory is so short that it is just wiped out of his consciousness, I don't know, though I doubt it. However, having just made him get down from my chair because of some particularly bad piece of behaviour, I will suddenly become aware that he is there again, snuggling in beside me. As often as not I am not even sure how long he has been there.

The strange thing is that while he seems to have this desire to get in beside the human beings, he very strongly objects to anyone trying to sit down beside *him*. On many occasions, seeing him curled up on the sofa, I have been overcome by the urge to sit down next to him, put my arms round him, and give him a cuddle. His response – to snarl and snap – I put down, the first time it happened, to his being caught unaware, perhaps in the middle of a dream. However, although since then I have tried to make sure that he is awake and aware of me before I approach him, the reaction invariably is the same – followed by his jumping down, going across to the chair I have usually just vacated, and snuggling down there!

My mother was fond of Rich Tea biscuits and of course Sam made sure he got what he considered to be his fair share of them. After she died, I felt it important this treat should be continued – the sudden loss of his beloved mistress was blow enough; to lose something he had become used to and almost certainly associated with her in his mind, seemed to me to be an extra and unnecessary cruelty. I continued to buy them, just for him, and usually gave him at least one a day.

This has resulted in another strange, not to say perverse, ritual that has seemed to become more extreme as time goes on. Normally, I will tend to be sitting down in my armchair when I hand the biscuit to him. His routine was, initially, to take it to his basket a few feet away opposite, dump it there, and then turn around and attack my feet! Even when I just threw it straight into his basket, he would go through the same act, going to it, then returning to have a go at my feet. More recently, when I have gone to the sideboard to fetch a biscuit, he has launched himself at my ankles, in what amounts to a rugby tackle, on my return.

Now, this is something that is not likely to be appreciated at the best of times – with my still deteriorating balance, even less so. What really puts the lid on it is the fact that as often as not the biscuit-ceremony occurs after a meal, when I have just placed a cup of tea on the coffee-table in front of my chair. As trying to negotiate my way between chair and table with Sam wrapped round my legs almost inevitably ends with my tea, not only spilt, but spilt over a highly polished surface, it is then that Sam's popularity with me reaches its virtual nadir!

Not surprisingly, my reaction eventually was to exclaim: 'Well, if that's the way you are going to behave you won't *have* a biscuit!' at the same time making a great display of putting the biscuit back in the packet and returning that to the sideboard, hoping that it would sink in that if he wanted to continue to receive this treat he was going to have to change his ways. *His* response involves him standing four-square in front of me, then circling round the table peering at me in what appears to be open-eyed astonishment, as he tries to take in this peculiar behaviour! 'What is he trying to do? – first he offers me a biscuit, then he takes it away and starts to shout at me! Really! What I have to put up with!' There is obviously no connection in his mind between his behaviour and my reaction. There has been, to date, no modification of this sequence of events.

Something similar often occurs when I feed him in the kitchen. After I have put his food down and try to sidle past him to return to the living-room, he will swing round and make swift darting movements at my feet. As I am often carrying my own food or drink, this performance again causes me great difficulty. The instinctive reaction – to kick out with my feet – is fatal, as he then grabs my ankle and attempts to shake it! How I have managed so far to avoid dropping anything or falling over, I don't know. How I have been able to keep myself from attempting to break his neck before he breaks mine, I have no idea.

Most of the paper-boys who come to the house nowadays accept Sam, as do the local children, who tend to laugh at him when he barks at them – though the younger ones sometimes scream and run a short distance in mock terror. However, in the past one or two have been nervous when they have seen him outside by the gate and have not wanted to pass him. On one occasion when I rang the newsagent to report that I hadn't yet received the local evening paper, I was told that neither had a number of other local people and until I called Sam in we weren't likely to! One boy in particular, an ex-pupil of mine, was, it seems, especially fearful of him, having apparently been bitten by another dog in the past. When I was made aware of this I went out of my way to try to ensure that Sam was in the house before the boy was due.

With this in mind, on this particular day I had just let him in the back door when the paper was pushed through the letter-box at the front. Sam, after going through his usual performance of rushing up to the door and barking furiously suddenly realised that the back door was still open and before I could do anything had turned and rushed past me. I heard a loud scream and reached the door in time to see the boy scrambling on hands and knees in his panic to get up the steep drive and away from Sam, who was snapping at his heels. They disappeared momentarily around the corner, Sam quickly re-emerging with a Yorkshire terrier's equivalent of a satisfied smile.

However, I don't think he inflicted any damage – if he had, I almost certainly would have been faced with repercussions of one kind or another. I can't remember if I ever saw the boy again or not – certainly he didn't last much longer anyway. Sam had a lot to answer for, in one way or another!

It was at about this time though that he received what could perhaps be described as his 'come-uppance'. I had on this afternoon just a few moments previously let him out the side door when I heard what sounded like a child's scream, followed by barking and a raised female voice, or voices. Knowing Sam's dislike of children, my instinctive reaction was to fear that the thing that I had been most dreading had occurred – he had attacked a young child. The fact that as I reached the door, he rushed past me with his tail between his legs seemed to confirm this. However, as I followed him into the living-room asking him what he had been doing, and calling him a bad dog in my assumption of the worst, I heard a female voice outside again.

'Is he all right? Has he been hurt? I tried to hold my dog off but he got away from me! It's the first time it's ever happened!'

Standing at the top of the drive was a young woman, struggling with a powerful dog – a Dobermann, I think – and looking very concerned. 'He grabbed your dog before I could stop him! I hope he's all right! Will you check and see?'

Returning to the living-room and examining Sam, cowering in his basket, it seemed obvious to me that although his coat was wet in parts – from where he had been in the Dobermann's mouth, presumably – no real damage had been done, no blood had been drawn. However, the young woman was still anxious to do the right thing, offering to take him to the local vet to have him checked over. There had been a great deal of publicity at that time about attacks by various big and aggressive dogs and calls for their control, if not banning, and she was obviously concerned that if I made a complaint it could result in trouble – for her and the dog.

There never was any likelihood of this, though. Knowing Sam, her description of what had happened was entirely believable and the consequences for Sam not deserving of sympathy. Apparently, as the Dobermann passed him he had followed closely, nipping at his heels. Whilst on previous occasions the Dobermann had accepted this on sufferance, this time he decided he had had enough and turned and grabbed him! It is perhaps lucky for Sam that the girl was strong enough finally to get her dog off him. It would have been unjust, not to say hypocritical, for me to have complained. It is only recently that it has occurred to me that I might anyway have been embarrassed to be called upon to explain what Sam was doing outside there without supervision.

He has always loved going out in the car and likes to have the rear window (nearside, for some reason) wound down. The sight of his little head stuck out, hair blown back by the wind, seems to be a source of great delight to pedestrains and occupants of passing cars alike. Again though, typically, having had that window opened, he will then move to the front seat and put his nose up to that window expecting *it* to be opened. Even though the car I have had in recent years has automatic windows, I soon tired of this.

I used to like to take him to open spaces to have a run around, taking great pleasure from his obvious enjoyment. Unfortunately, two factors – one, his tendency to disappear into the distance, leaving me waiting, straining for a glimpse of him until he eventually reappeared, usually trailing another dog; the other, the increasing introduction of notices of anti-pollution bye-laws and the use of dog-wardens to implement them, made things difficult. The fact that he also on occasion lost his bearings and nearly found his way on to the road was the thing that eventually brought about the end of these runs.

I was surprised to find that even though a trip now usually meant just being left in the car while I did my shopping and sometimes had lunch or a snack out, he still showed great eagerness whenever he thought I was getting ready to go out. This perhaps contains the clue towards explaining the surprising addition to the Sam fan club of two taxi-drivers who had the job of transporting him on different occasions to and from the local kennels. From a firm regularly engaged by the kennels for this purpose, they each spontaneously exclaimed on handing him over on his return: 'What a lovely dog!'

Could this be the Sam I knew and loved? Certainly, this was something new and unexpected – particularly as, on the first occasion, I had been slightly concerned as to how he would behave. But no, there was no doubt – they both almost fell over themselves to express their admiration, bending over at the door to pat and stroke him as I let him in. They said how quietly he had sat and been no bother at all. 'Why,' said the second, 'he sat on my lap all the way!' I put aside any mental query as to the advisability of this, happy to accept the new experience. Previously, the best that was said of him related to his looks: 'What a pretty face he has!' by the proprietress of the kennels and one or two others.

The reaction of the drivers is perhaps based on their previous encounters with passengers of the canine variety when carried alone. I can imagine that some of the larger dogs particularly can be a bit of a problem. Fearing the worst when receiving a call to make another collection, I suppose Sam – a small dog who sat more or less quietly – must have seemed pretty-well angelic.

Sometimes, on one of these trips with him, I would visit an ex-colleague who lived locally. Her house was very close to Brighton & Hove Albion Football Stadium and on the day of a 'home' match the roads all around would be packed with cars. Normally, I tried to make sure I avoided these occasions, but on this particular Saturday I had not checked and arrived to find that the only space left was on a double yellow line near a corner. There were a policeman and policewoman there, standing beside a lamppost and as I approached I pointed to the spot indicating where I wanted to park, as a holder of an orange badge. They responded with sweeping gestures that suggested: 'Be our guest.'

As I opened the door to let Sam out, he rushed past me and, in a great curve, made for the lamppost. It would make a better story to say that he peed down the WPC's leg, but, while he didn't actually do so, he couldn't have missed by more than a couple of centimetres! As I hurried to get away into my friend's house, looking anxiously over my shoulder, I saw that both 'police-persons' were grinning from ear to ear in apparent delight. It probably was the one bright spot in a generally boring day for them.

He usually came with me when I drove over to visit another friend, at Burwash. Mike was not Sam's biggest fan, in that he took great pride in his back garden and didn't appreciate Sam's tendency on release to head for one of his most treasured plants, cock his leg, and subject it to an unwelcome watering. When you add to this the fact that he doesn't like dogs anyway, you can perhaps understand that Sam was only accepted on sufferance and was grabbed and tied to a heavy garden bench before he could make a move! However, Mike was very kind in that he was prepared to take him for short walks while we were there.

On one particular occasion, we had driven a little way into the countryside and pulled in to a layby in a narrow, winding lane. Mike said he would take the dog a short distance round the corner, where there was a field ideal for exercising him, and where he could get rid of anything he needed to before we returned home. As they set off, with Sam trotting along, apparently quite happily, on his lead, I lay back comfortably in the car awaiting their return, thinking in terms of 20 to 30 minutes.

Sam was the first to reappear, within about three minutes, at full pelt – dragging his lead behind him. Next to emerge from around the corner, demonstrating a high-knee lift and co-ordinated arm action that would have met with the full approval of the television athletics commentators (even if the red, contorted face wouldn't), was Mike – followed in turn by a line of about six cars. The occupants, suddenly having revealed to them what it was that had been holding them up, were universally showing their delight at the spectacle. Mike alone was the only one present not enjoying the situation. It seems that things had been all right until he was trying to open a gate to let Sam into the field. Sam, with his usual awkwardness, decided this was his opportunity to break away and get back to the car. It hardly needs saying that Mike's public discomfiture at Sam's hands (paws?) didn't do anything to increase his regard for him, even though he has since taken him for walks again.

Someone else who was sufficiently tolerant to give him another chance lived to regret it. George, the fellow writer whose kindness was earlier rejected by Sam, decided for some reason or other to try again. He made a point on these short excursions of directing him towards the gutter to relieve himself. Sam complied with this for the first couple of times then, typically, decided suddenly to do his own thing – heading back on to the pavement and doing a job by someone's gate before George could do anything about it. It fits in with one of those immutable laws of life that this was the moment for the occupier to appear, exclaim: 'So *that's* the dog that has been fouling the pavement outside my house!' and stalk off. Poor George was too taken aback by the injustice of this to feel able to respond. He made it clear on his return, however, that that *really was* the last time!

Having to resort to letting Sam out the front again, I began to feel that the neighbours were now accepting it – particularly considering that since my mother had died he tended to stay out for such a short time. However, this illusion was short-lived, as one day I suddenly received a letter from someone living opposite complaining that, he/she had just watched Sam excrete outside their house, and threatening action if it occurred again. As it wasn't signed but just gave a house number, which made replying difficult (was I to say Dear Number –?) I decided just to let it go.

I heard nothing for some time and had almost forgotten about it, when I got another, from the same address, this time signed. 'Mrs-'. I felt I had to answer this, to impress upon her the particular factors that made things so difficult and all I had tried to do to get over the problem. I went out of my way to be conciliatory, expressing my regret, offering my apologies and hoping she would understand that, whatever else, it wasn't done out of thoughtlessness or lack of consideration. Again, I heard nothing for some time and again I began to feel that the situation had been more or less accepted and my difficulties acknowledged. This too however turned out to be an illusion.

One day, out of the blue, following portentous knocking at the back door, the local Dog Warden presented himself to say that neighbours – or one in particular – had been complaining about Sam. He pointed out a notice, recently placed on a lamppost right outside my house, warning that allowing dogs to foul the pavement was an offence punishable by a fine. (I must admit I had seen it being put up and had experienced a feeling of guilt – thinking that it was directed to me – or Sam and me – personally.) Whilst he assured me that this was not so; they were going up all over Brighton, he warned me that something would have to be done about it. Though he took a very understanding viewpoint and said he was determined to resist any suggestion that I should be prosecuted, he was talking in terms of finding a new home for Sam, through the PDSA. Because of the tough stance taken by that one neighbour in particular, he felt that his own job was at risk unless he stopped Sam's activities.

For a time I almost considered letting Sam go – if nothing else, it would make for an easier, less stressful life – but the more I thought about it, the more I turned against the idea. However difficult he made it for me, the alternative of a Sam-less existence was something I didn't want to contemplate. I felt that if I submitted and let him go I would almost certainly soon regret it. The thought of going out in the car without him next to me or, even worse, returning from a trip and his not being there, in the house when I got in was depressing in the extreme. The fact that I was told the decision, once taken, was irrevocable and that I would never be allowed to see him again was the deciding factor. The idea just couldn't be entertained! It may have just been my rationalising to say that I couldn't anyway see any elderly lady coping with Sam, but I really couldn't.

Finally, because of the problems involved in trying to put him into the back garden, I fell back on the idea of an extended lead into the front garden – a rough and ready affair, but at least it worked, within its limits. Of course, Sam *being* Sam, one of the first things he did was to wind himself, or his lead, around a conveniently placed tree! Its rough bark resisted the lead just being pulled free, simply fraying the thick string of which it was partly constructed, and causing me eventually to have to go out, usually in pyjamas and dressing-gown, to try to release him. Fortunately, he largely gave that up after a while but that still left the problem of my having to go out and remove the mess from the path where he initially tended to deposit it – with my precarious balance, hazardous in the extreme!

Again though, typically of Sam, he suddenly, for reasons best known to himself decided to change tack and go (in both meanings of the word) around the corner of the front porch, on the crazy-paving. Apart from the fact that this made it so much more difficult to get at, he also now managed to get his lead round the other side of a row of recently planted ornamental Chinese cabbage. He would then stare through the glass side of the porch, apparently unable to move, and start barking. To avoid having to risk life and limb by going outside to him, I tended to just pull on my end of the rope/lead. One by one, the ornamental cabbage have thus been uprooted, until now there is only one, standing forlornly in silent accusation! It is perhaps as well that I wasn't over-enamoured of them in the first place.

It comes as a shock to realise, by thinking back, how relatively old Sam now is in canine terms. Remembering that when he was bought in 1981 he was already ten months old, in 1994 he is around fourteen – well into what should be his 'declining years'. Other people express surprise; there is little about his physical appearance or behaviour to suggest advancing age. It is only very recently that a couple of giveaways have appeared to pull one up with a jolt: even Sam isn't immortal!

The first thing I noticed was a decline in his jumping ability. In his early days it was quite common for him, not only to jump onto the arms of our lounge-suite and stand there but also to get onto the backs of any armchair anyone happened to be sitting in at the time. Whilst this latter feat was normally achieved in two stages, he sometimes suddenly appeared standing behind and above one, having leapt from a standing position on the carpet – a considerable performance bearing in mind the size of the suite; and of Sam!

One of the saddest sights now is of Sam trying to jump on to the sofa, scrabbling for a moment as he attempts to hold on, then slowly slipping back. However, he is not easily defeated and usually now stands there wiggling his bottom from side to side as he tries to gear himself up to have another go. Eventually, so far, he manages to get there. He seems more or less though to have given up trying to get on to the bed in what was my mother's bedroom. I tend often to lie down there in the afternoon and Sam sometimes manages to open the door and get in, making immediately for the bed. I should really have appreciated the fact he generally finds it impossible now and been thankful for it, but at times my misplaced compassion caused me to grab him by the collar as he was tensing himself for the jump and haul him up. The fact that I came close to strangling him in the process may go some way to explaining why he seems recently to have lost interest in the whole idea.

Another manifestation of the effects of the passage of time relates to his stance on passing water. In the past he aroused some amusement – amounting in the case of one female ex-colleague almost to hysteria – by his tendency to throw one of his hind legs vertically in the air and hold it there, like a ballet-dancer on points. Nowadays, he normally just stands with his four legs slightly spread and simply lets it pour out. Perhaps an early sign of the encroachment of rheumatism?

The fact that sooner or later I would be faced with the death of Sam is something of which I have been aware for some time. Although it has mainly been pushed into my sub-conscious, it has been brought to the surface on a number of occasions through the years when I was confronted with the possibility of losing him. The most obvious of these, I suppose, were the times when he had to be taken in to the surgery overnight and anaesthetised for pretty drastic work on his teeth. On the last of these occasions, having despatched someone to collect him afterwards, expecting their return within a few minutes, I became more and more apprehensive as hour followed hour and I heard nothing.

Finally, absolutely certain that the only possible explanation was that he had died under the anaesthetic and they were trying to bring themselves to break the news to me, I took my courage in my hands and phoned the surgery to confirm the worst. I cannot remember now exactly what was the reason given for the delay, but they couldn't understand my pessimistic state. 'No,' I was assured, 'he's fine! He'll be back shortly.'

In between these times, there was a real scare for me when Sam, on being let out one morning, collapsed, as he went down the step in to the front porch and just lay there stretched out on his stomach, seeming unable to move. After making a tentative attempt to help him up, I decided to leave him where he was and ring the vet. Seeming to think it may have been due to some kind of heart condition he suggested leaving him for the moment to see if he would get up by himself. Eventually, he did but the episode implanted a worry in my mind and for some time I was half-expecting a repeat, but with more serious results. Whilst I never witnessed such a thing, I seem to remember a similar collapse being reported by someone who had charge of him in recent years.

Bearing in mind my own health problems, mostly connected directly or indirectly with the so-called post-polio syndrome, it was seeming to become a question as to which of us would go first – with, at times, all the signs of it being 'a pretty close-run thing'. I found myself considering which alternative would be the better – from the point of view of the one left behind. While I have earlier stated my apprehension as to the effect the loss of Sam would have on me, I came to the conclusion that it was perhaps preferable that it should happen that way round rather than the other.

This feeling derived primarily from his reaction to the death of my mother – something that has been held in my memory since. He was of course her dog, and she – from what we are told of dog psychology – 'belonged' to *him*. My mother had been ill for a couple of days and Sam had been on her bed when a succession of doctors had called, the last one arranging her admission to hospital. Sam had made it very difficult for them to examine her. The ambulancemen he resisted ferociously, snapping and snarling as they got her out of bed and took her away.

Obviously Sam would have realised something was wrong, even if he didn't have the sort of extrasensory perception said sometimes to be possessed by animals. As time passed and his mistress didn't reappear be became more and more withdrawn and miserable-looking. I was still teaching then so was away for a large part of the day through the week. Most evenings when I came home he seemed to be in the same chair he had been in when I left in the morning. Although very occasionally he would rouse himself sufficiently to wander out and sniff at me on my return, he would then wearily make his way back to his chair and flop himself down again. Most of the time though he hardly acknowledged me at all, restricting himself to a baleful glare over his shoulder. He seemed to be eating virtually nothing.

My mother died suddenly and, to me, unexpectedly,

within two days of her admission to hospital. The saddest and most affecting thing that followed occurred when I brought her belongings home some time later. Sam hadn't come to the hospital with me and, when he heard me let myself in to the kitchen, had come through to investigate. As I put the case down I had anticipated what would happen next. Sam went up to it and after sniffing it tentatively, began to wag his tail. Although it was my suitcase and had only been used by my mother for this one special purpose, and although it remained shut with her things sealed inside, he obviously identified it with her and concluded she would be following.

I sat beside him in the armchair with the suitcase nearby and tried to explain to him that she had gone and wouldn't be returning, but although I (naively perhaps) almost convinced myself that some of it at least had got through, I have suspected that in the years since he has been expecting her suddenly to reappear. Thinking about this, I have wondered to whom in those circumstances he would go. Certainly, in the period immediately following her death, there is little or no doubt – she would have been restored naturally and without question to her original position as the recipient of his absolute devotion. I try to convince myself that as time has gone by this has at least become less sure.

The purpose behind my relating this is to make the point that with Sam already having suffered the loss of one owner – almost certainly still not fully recovered from – for him to lose her replacement, and the only thing that remained to connect him to her, would I feel be unsustainable, once he had taken in what had happened. As I think it likely that the family of a boy who had been at the school where I used to teach would take him over, at least initially, in the event of my death, I suspect that for some time he would just accept the situation and not be concerned.

They had taken him over on a number of occasions recently when I was away or unwell. He was always made a fuss of and given the kind of exercise I was unable to give him.

However, I hope I am not flattering myself in feeling that after a while he would begin to become aware that something was missing and to wonder when he was going to be returned to where he belonged – the place he was used to and where he had lived with my mother and me. While he seemed quite happy to go with these people, he would hold at least a subconscious awareness from previous experience that sooner or later he was always brought back. Those bringing him used to comment on the way in which he tended to drag them down the drive when they let him out of the car: 'He certainly knows where he lives, doesn't he?' was a constant remark. When he was brought to the front door, and I went in answer to the knock to let him in, Sam's little face would be seen, his nose pressed eagerly against the glass panel.

Certainly, I was always conscious of how severely I would be affected by the reverse situation, as indicated earlier in giving my reasons for rejecting the idea of letting him be taken over by the PDSA. Nevertheless, I feel that one essential difference in the two cases justifies my preferred alternative. That relates to the fact that although we both would be aware in our different ways of our loss, I at least would have some understanding of, and control over, events. Whilst it would be some time before Sam began to take things in, in his limited consciousness, I feel that his very lack of understanding and particularly of control makes him that much more vulnerable. His suffering eventually would be the greater and, I believe, would build up through the years.

He was becoming more and more dependent. Strangely, it was my cleaner who brought to my attention the fact that he was tending to follow me around much more than he used to. She would call out to me when I was in the bathroom to tell me that Sam was waiting patiently outside as close to the door as he could manage. A little earlier, the vet had made official something I had been at least half-aware of, having noticed for some time Sam's increasing tendency to bump into things and his lack of response to my voice when I was standing behind him, even quite closely sometimes. Often I would approach him, calling all the while, when he was standing with his nose pressed against one of the doors, apparently thinking I was inside. Only when I touched him with my foot would he turn with a start to find me there.

He was, apparently, now almost blind – through cataracts – and deaf. Often, I would come on him in the hall just standing there, as if unable to move. It was almost as if he didn't know where he was. It occurs to me now just how vulnerable he must have felt. The vet had said that nothing could be done about the cataracts, but whether that meant that it was physically impossible, too dangerous, or just not worthwhile I don't know. If I had thought it possible and made some kind of sense I would have been prepared to pay, to make life better for him, if only for a short while. In the light of subsequent events I suppose it would have been virtually pointless, though.

* * *

Sam's death when it occurred was, due to the unfortunate circumstances surrounding it, even more devastating in its effect on me than it otherwise might have been. Although he had been unwell for some days, there seemed little to indicate that it was anything more to worry about than his many previous bouts of ill health. It wasn't until the last 48 hours or so that things began to look a little more serious.

Even then, the end, in its manner and suddenness came as a great shock.

About a year previously I had noticed some kind of swelling on the right side of his upper lip, immediately under his nose. The vet seemed unsure as to what it was, though he suggested it was some form of tumour. Its close proximity to the nose apparently precluded any possibility of surgical removal and, as an alternative, he sent back with the boy who had taken him in, a tube of ointment with instructions to rub some in five times a day! Bearing in mind the fact that, through a traumatic experience when trying to examine him on a home visit, Mr Pepper knew what that was likely to involve, I had felt I wanted to ask if he had been smiling when he said it!

While there was no possibility of my being able to carry out this procedure five times a day, I did manage to apply the ointment a couple of times on the first day – talk about the quickness of the hand deceiving the snapping jaws – but it became increasingly difficult as time went by even to get him to come near enough for me to get at him. I thought I did fairly well if I managed it once a day. The only positive thing was that it was obvious to me, from his lack of reaction when the ointment was actually being applied, that neither the act, nor apparently therefore the lump, was painful. However, the fact that I had to grasp his collar so hard to prevent him from turning his head to bite me caused both of us to fear I was going to choke him!

Considering that I was able to apply it so infrequently, it came as some surprise that after a short while the size of the lump seemed to be reduced until eventually that side of his upper lip appeared to have returned to the same size as the other. Feeling considerably relieved, I was distressed when it reappeared, this time looking painfully red and raw. However, from that previous experience, I was less concerned than I otherwise would have been, consoling myself with the thought that although the problem of application was now to be repeated, it could be hoped it would meet with the same success as before. When I suggested to the vet though that the fact that the previous lump had been reduced showed at least it wasn't a tumour, I was somewhat disconcerted to be told that it was not necessarily so.

Actually, although this (as I then thought) new one looked so much more dreadful than before, things went very much as they had the first time. While there was still the same difficulty rubbing the ointment on, at least it remained possible. Again, it seemed to cause Sam no pain and, more surprising, once it was started he seemed prepared to remain standing quietly, while it was gently rubbed in. As before too, even though he tended immediately to lick it off there seemed to be a gradual but definite improvement. I began to feel quite optimistic that things were going to be all right after all.

Sam had always liked to share my morning toast but for some time had rejected pieces of crust or anything that was at all hard, just dropping them on the carpet. Therefore I had begun to chew his toast before offering it to him and he had again accepted it happily. Now, however, he suddenly started rejecting even this. Because of his obvious difficulty with chewing generally, I had for some months previously been buying ordinary mince (not pet-mince) from the butcher, which we shared. After a period when he was turning away from virtually everything offered, he so eagerly wolfed it down I thought at least part of his dietary problems had been solved. It came as a great shock when he turned away from this too. Making it even more worrying was the fact that he still kept confronting me expectantly as if he was sure I would produce something for him that he *could* eat.

When he started being sick, my first thought was that it

was probably a result of his ingestion of the ointment he had been licking off his face, though the vet's assistant I consulted on the phone thought it unlikely. What amazed me was the amount and appearance of what he brought up – fairly largish yellow lumps, when the only food put down for him previously was a small piece of chicken which he hardly seemed to touch anyway. He seemed now to be deteriorating fairly rapidly and I was becoming increasingly concerned.

Things came to a head when I was woken early one morning by Sam scratching at my bedroom door. He had obviously been ill during the night and was just standing there, apparently unable to move. He was in an awful state, with a string of saliva hanging from his mouth and a mess of blood and excrement around his anus. Plainly, the vet had to be brought in to him, whatever the expense. Meanwhile, I thought that the only thing I could do was to put his water-bowl under his nose, in the hope that he would at least drink something. In the event, I don't think he did.

The vet reported that Sam had a temperature of 106F, but said that at least a very high temperature was preferable to a very low one – which tended to indicate the animal's system had given up. He gave him an injection, which he hoped would restore his temperature to normal, and asked for him to be brought in to the surgery the following afternoon for checking, when it would have had time to have taken effect.

That night I was woken twice by Sam alternately squealing and groaning, causing me to have to go out and attempt to comfort him. He was hanging half out of his basket, which was in the hall opposite my door. I managed to persuade and ease him back into it, but from then on he spent his time crawling out and flopping down on the hall carpet and then crawling back in again. A large part of the time though he spent half in and half out, as I had found him during the night.

Now began an unfortunate, and for me tragic, series of events, with everything seeming to happen for the worst. Having previously arranged for the newspaper boy to take Sam in to the surgery in the afternoon, as the vet had requested, it was now obvious that it was too much of an emergency for such a delay in his being seen. The boy very kindly agreed to take him to the morning surgery instead — luckily, as it was during the school holidays, being available to do so — agreeing to forego something he had been intending to do.

By an appalling piece of bad luck, his arrival at the door coincided with a torrential downpour. Normally, I would almost certainly have suggested he returned later but in the circumstances I didn't think I could. After his kindness in agreeing to take Sam at all and then to change the time and take him in earlier, it seemed to me that it would be asking too much. Even if he had agreed I feel that his parents, seeing him return home already drenched, would have protested on being told he had to go out again.

The trouble was that this was a situation I hadn't anticipated — it wasn't until I opened the door to him that I discovered that it was raining at all, let alone that it was torrential. I vaguely felt that somewhere in the house was a plastic mac, which would have been almost ideal to cover him with, but I wasn't sure where it was and didn't feel capable of finding it at a moment's notice. If I'd had forewarning, I might have been able to locate it and have it ready. Again, to add to the list of regrets and what-might-have-beens, the previous time Shaun had carried Sam to the surgery, he had rejected the offer of a large and strong plastic bag with a cushion in the bottom as a means of carrying him, preferring to hold him just wrapped in a towel.

It is so easy after the event to go over and torture oneself with the things which suddenly seem clear but which at the time were either confused by circumstances or didn't occur at all. The idea to put Sam into the plastic bag did enter my mind but influenced by its previous rejection and also, it must be admitted, by the fact that I was not even sure where it was now, it just passed out again. Then again, it occurred to me later that I could have suggested that Shaun came inside and waited, in the hope that the storm would ease off. The question there is whether he and/or his parents would have been happy at the idea.

The result was that Sam was again carried just wrapped in a towel and was absolutely drenched – so much so that the vet asked later if he had been dropped in a bath! Although they said they dried him thoroughly with a towel (in Sam's state, an ordeal in itself, I would have thought) I find it difficult to convince myself that the whole incident didn't contribute to the final outcome. The fact that Sam was now reported as having the very low temperature that I had been told was such a bad sign, is particularly hard to dissociate in my mind from his experience, however much I would like to. In all this, the thing that causes me the greatest unhappiness – not to say bitterness – is that the downpour that started so suddenly, to coincide with Sam's being collected, ended just as suddenly within 15 or 20 minutes. It almost seemed as if there was some evil spirit, or influence, out to cause poor Sam the greatest harm possible.

What followed fitted in completely with all that had gone before on that day. When Sam had been taken in I had been told, as far as I can remember, to leave it until early evening to check how he was. Being very concerned, I decided to phone in about mid-afternoon. It was then just after 3 o'clock and in the middle of their special surgery. I spoke to a female assistant, who seemed happy to assure me that Sam, although obviously still not well was now much brighter and looking around almost perkily. The sense of relief I felt at this was short-lived. Within a quarter of an hour, just as I was lowering myself onto the bed, suddenly overcome by tiredness, the telephone rang. I had a terrible premonition as to what it was.

The male caller introduced himself as one of the vets at the surgery – not the one I knew but another member of the practice. He said he had just gone into the room where Sam was and found him in the middle of a fit, following which he just lay there quivering. 'I must tell you,' he said, 'if he were my dog, I would have him put down.' He went on to make it clear that he thought that any delay in taking action would just extend Sam's suffering.

This put me in a truly awful dilemma. In considering through the years the likelihood, if not inevitability, of my being faced with this situation eventually, I had always promised myself that I would be there with Sam when it was done, to try to reassure him. To be able to put my hand on him and speak to him I thought might prevent his becoming frightened. However, the fact that I was confronted with this so suddenly after having my mind put at rest and as I was then, having just lain down, feeling unwell and still in pyjamas and dressing-gown, I didn't think I could face it. My belief at the time that even if I could get a taxi fairly quickly, it would mean my having to go through a crowded surgery in such a state, was an added factor against. It wasn't until much later that I began to realise that it was as the surgery was coming to an end that the vet had rung.

When I told him of the promise I had made myself and my doubts about my ability to fulfil it, he said that, while he could perhaps bring Sam to me for it to be done it would just increase and prolong his suffering. This was so obviously true that I felt that I had to agree to let him go ahead with it there. In the time since, I have had no doubt about this decision – after all, the overwhelming priority was to do what was best for Sam and from what I learned from the vet about the condition that led to him having to be put down, it seems obvious that even if he had recovered from that immediate crisis it would soon have been replaced by another. The evil day could not long be delayed.

Apparently Sam had an 'incursive tumour', of which the obvious part was the lump under his nose, but which it seems connected up in some way I don't understand with a hole in his mouth that had failed to heal after a tooth extraction. Although I was told no more than this, it would seem to be the reason for his crying out and moaning on that final night. While the lump had appeared not to have caused him pain earlier, it is well-known in human cases that often it is not until the later stages that pain arises. Now, apparently, that stage had been reached with Sam. As the two things that had led to him having to be put down — the direct physical effect of his suffering and the resulting indirect effect on his ability to eat — would remain and perhaps worsen, the inevitable had to be faced, for his sake.

The unhappiness that remains relates to the sense of guilt I still feel about my failure to be there with him when the time came. I cannot escape the feeling of my having betrayed him, let him down. I should have been there — I owed it to him. Although the vet tried to convince me that my presence would have made no difference, that Sam probably would not have been aware of me, I find it hard to take it in and accept it. Perhaps I have a subconscious need to punish myself. It occurred to me later that as far as Sam would have been aware, there would have been no difference between the injection he was given to put him down and those he was given before the two operations on his teeth — the only variant being the amount of anaesthetic used. This, in a perverse way, made me feel better about things. After all, I reminded myself, I had not been with him on those occasions either. Unfortunately, my logic didn't allow me to enjoy the luxury of this sop to my conscience for long. Couldn't it be looked at from the opposite viewpoint – that I had also let him down on those previous occasions?

I was asked by the vet if I wanted his collar returned. Although I felt I needed time to consider it, I think there was probably never really any doubt that I would ask for it back – I could after all, I told myself, get rid of it later if I began to feel differently about it. Thinking ahead, I was at least vaguely aware that if I let it go then, that would be it. No amount of wishing or regrets would bring it back. Not only do I still have it, but his basket is still there outside the living-room door as also are the yellow stains just in front of it, on the hall carpet.

Through the years, the carpet had accumulated quite a few stains – almost all connected with Sam and his bodily functions. Whenever the question of cleaning or replacing it came up the idea was rejected, as I realised it would soon be rendered pointless. As long as Sam remained, the staining would recur. His death might have seemed to have been the opportunity to do what had been needed for so long. I think that momentarily I did consider it but the idea was instantly dismissed. The carpet, and particularly the evidence of his last illness, was, with his basket, virtually my only remaining connection with Sam. I didn't feel I could let either go – not yet, anyway.

Of all the things associated with Sam's illnesses, something that made perhaps the greatest impression on me was, strangely enough, wording I spotted on a little box from the vet. In the space labelled 'name', appeared 'Sam Mason-Apps'. Now, I don't know if this is simply the standard way of labelling pet-medicines – certainly it would seem a logical way of doing it. I can only say that I had not consciously encountered it before. The fact that Sam was hereby officially given the status of family member, I found strangely, immensely, touching. Should he be regarded as my brother, or son? Even before his death I had made a mental note that it was something I would have to keep.

One of the first things I did after his death was to look for the last such box that had arrived. This, containing ointment for his nose, I remembered seeing on the coffee-table in front of my armchair, where it had been kept to be easily available for application. It was not there! I assumed that my cleaner, thinking that as Sam was now dead I wouldn't want to keep it, had simply thrown it out. Desperately unhappy, I was divided between annoyance with my cleaner and bitter anger with myself. After all, while it could be considered a reasonable reaction on Ann's part to feel it best to get rid of it (though I would have hoped that she would have asked me first), my failure either to tell her of my desire to keep it, or to put it somewhere safe, but instead to think vaguely in terms of doing it later, was a typical piece of downright stupidity for which I cursed myself unmercifully.

Then, looking round the room in desperation but with little or no hope, I spotted something on one of the bookshelves opposite me – a small narrow cardboard box! With some excitement I rushed across the room and grabbed it, not really daring to believe it could be what I was looking for. The label read 'Sam Mason-Apps'! I still had it! It had not been thrown out! In fact, it turned out later that it wasn't the box I had been looking for, but an earlier one that had apparently been put aside. The one that I had left on the table I discovered a couple of days afterwards on the Welsh dresser – again, it seems, put there to be safe. So I had, not one, but two!

Although the re-discovery of these boxes and, more

important, their labels, produced some lightening of the blackness that had descended on me, still I felt suddenly in great need of companionship and comforting. After all, Sam and I had shared our lives for fourteen years and had been all each other had for the last nine of these. At times in those first one or two days after his death I even thought in terms of contacting the Samaritans, so great was my sense of loss. While I put that idea from my mind, I did ring my GP. However, when I told his secretary that I didn't want to be prescribed tranquillisers, she suggested that would be all he would be able to offer. Thinking about it, I had to agree that seemed logical and just let the idea go. I wasn't sure what I *did* want — probably just to be visited and talked to.

That was in my mind when I contacted one or two other people who knew Sam — and me, of course. Two of them: the ex-colleague with the large garden who had been so kind to him in the past; and George's son Richard did just that, volunteering to come round to sit with me and talk. Their kindness and understanding over the following days made all the difference to my state of mind. Perhaps most important to me, neither tried to play down the importance of what had happened — to suggest, 'Ah well! very sad, but he was only a *pet* after all.' Richard especially, having lost his father equally suddenly a short time prior to this, might have been expected to react in such a way. In such a close-knit, loving family — with he and his sister now left alone after the earlier death of their mother, it would have been entirely understandable. However, if there was the slightest hint of this in his feelings, it never for a moment showed. His sympathy and understanding seemed complete, and genuine.

Sally, the ex-colleague, living nearer and having a car, was of particular help. For some time previously, long before Sam's death, I had been considering moving back to Hove, where we – my mother, stepfather and myself – had a flat before coming to Woodingdean. There were a number of factors involved: even before my mother died, this house, a four-bedroom chalet bungalow, was too large; being purchased hurriedly through a certain combination of circumstances. With her death, it really made no kind of sense at all. Then, Woodingdean being very hilly made it increasingly difficult for me to get about, while Hove – particularly the area where we used to live and where I thought of returning – is flat. If one adds to these points the fact that also in this area is the main shopping street, where virtually every kind of retailer – and eating-place – can be found, the arguments in favour of such a move are obvious.

Sally resurrected the idea and offered to drive me round to local estate agents to collect details of what suitable properties were available. From these, we selected those that seemed most promising from the point of view of accessibility, price etc, with the idea of following them up later. However, although I am still keeping this in mind, I have not so far brought myself to do so. Unfortunately, while in the abstract the idea of my moving has obvious appeal, when it comes down to actually making the decision one is presented with a terrible paradox.

Following Sam's death, it could be suggested that in moving, one would be leaving behind sad memories. The thing that strikes me though is that, in effect, I would also be leaving behind Sam. To add to the paradox, while moving – both the physical act and the having to get used to unfamiliar surroundings – would always present something of a trauma, doing so with Sam would at least be sustainable; doing so without him was impossible to contemplate. While the loss of Sam was a fact that had to be accepted, the loss of all the things that connected him to me, or me to him, was not. Nor did I feel prepared to make the attempt.

I remain intensely grateful to Sally for what she did for me and hope she understands it was not wasted effort. Even if none of the properties we saw is ever taken up by me the benefit was at least two-fold; firstly, in taking me out of myself and giving me something else to think about for a short time: secondly, in making me aware of what was available and therefore putting me in a position to make a comparison between it and what I presently have, for future reference. I suppose though that it was a combination of these things, including the opportunity to sit and have lunch again in the same Hove hamburger bar I used to visit regularly on my trips with Sam. The overall effect made all the difference to me.

Some years ago, not long after my mother died, her friend (the one who lived to regret offering to look after Sam while I was in hospital) suddenly exclaimed during one of my regular visits with him to her flat, 'My gosh! You would miss him, wouldn't you?' At a time when my conscious awareness of Sam was mainly of the negative side of being left to cope with him – the problem of exercising him, his awkwardness and general perversity – this had the effect of pulling me up with a start. What *would* I do? Would I miss him? Of course I would! How could I have survived without him? As I was to say many times later, it was his very awkwardness, and sometimes outright naughtiness, that made Sam his lovable self.

Thinking back now, I can only say: 'My gosh, Sam, I miss you!'